Fifth Disease

Elizabeth Laskey

Designed by Patricia Stevenson
Printed and bound in the United States by Lake Book Manufacturing

07 06 05 04 03
10 9 8 7 6 5 4 3 2 1

Library of Congress Cataloging-in-Publication Data
Laskey, Elizabeth, 1961–
    Fifth disease / Elizabeth Laskey.
        v. cm. — (It's catching)
    Includes bibliographical references and index.
    Contents: What is fifth disease? — How it got its name —
    What causes fifth disease? — First signs — The rash breaks out —
    The rash clears up — How fifth disease is spread — Who gets fifth disease? —
    Treatment — When it's more serious — Avoiding fifth disease —
    Staying healthy — Think about it.
    ISBN 1-4034-0272-8
    1. Fifth disease—Juvenile literature. [1. Fifth disease. 2. Diseases.]
    I. Title. II. Series.

RL271 .L37 2002
616.5—dc21
                            2001008560

Acknowledgments
The author and publishers are grateful to the following for permission to reproduce copyright material:
Cover photograph by Ken Greer/Visuals Unlimited
p. 4 Visuals Unlimited; p. 5 Bob Daemmrich/Stock Boston, Inc.; pp. 6, 7 Bettmann/Corbis; p. 8 Gelderblom/Eye of Science/Photo Researchers, Inc.; p. 9 Philip James Corwin/Corbis; p. 10 Billy E. Barnes/PhotoEdit/PictureQuest; p. 11 Tom Stewart/Corbis Stock Market; p. 12 Ken Greer/Visuals Unlimited; pp. 13, 14 Logical Images/Custom Medical Stock Photo; p. 15 Myrleen Cate/Photo Network/PictureQuest; p. 16 Reflections Photo Library/Corbis; pp. 17, 20 Bob Daemmrich/Stock Boston, Inc./PictureQuest; p. 18 Barbara J. Feigles/Stock Boston, Inc.; p. 19 Dan McCoy/Rainbow/PictureQuest; p. 21 Corbis; p. 22 Meckes/Ottawa/Photo Researchers, Inc.; p. 23 Michael Keller/Corbis Stock Market; p. 24 David Young-Wolff/PhotoEdit/PictureQuest; p. 25 Charles Gupton/Stock Boston, Inc./PictureQuest; p. 26 Photo Researchers, Inc.; p. 27 Camille Tokerud/Photo Researchers, Inc.; p. 28 Margaret Ross/Stock Boston, Inc.; p. 29 Tara Fulton/Visuals Unlimited.
Every effort has been made to contact copyright holders of any material reproduced in this book. Any omissions will be rectified in subsequent printings if notice is given to the publisher.

Some words are shown in bold, **like this.** You can find out what they mean by looking in the glossary.

Contents

What Is Fifth Disease?

Fifth disease is a sickness that gives you bright red patches on your cheeks. These patches are called a **rash.** The rash may also be on other parts of your body.

Fifth disease is an **infectious** illness. This means it can spread from one person to another.

How it Got its Name

Fifth disease got its name about 100 years ago. At that time, doctors looked at how children's sicknesses were the same and different from each other.

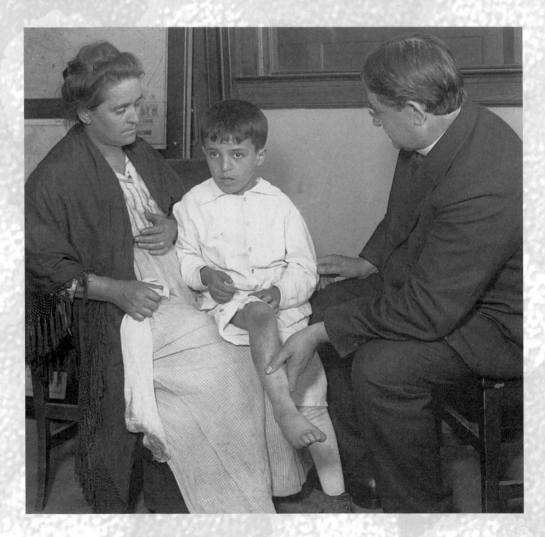

They put the sicknesses that cause **rashes** into one group. The illness that we call fifth disease was the fifth sickness they listed in that group.

What Causes Fifth Disease?

Fifth disease is caused by a **virus.** A virus is a tiny **germ** that can make you sick. A virus can only be seen through a **microscope.** This is what fifth disease viruses look like through a microscope.

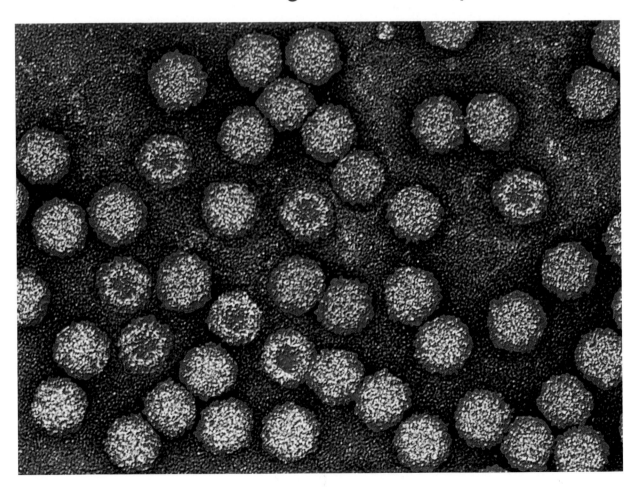

If the fifth disease virus gets into your body, it can make many more viruses. When this happens, you get sick.

First Signs

The first signs of fifth disease feel a lot like having a cold. You may have a runny or stuffy nose. Your head may hurt. You may also feel tired and have a **fever.**

When you have a fever, your body's **temperature** is hotter than normal. A fever is one way your body fights **infection.**

The Rash Breaks Out

After you have fifth disease for about a week, a **rash** will break out. You will see red patches on your cheeks.

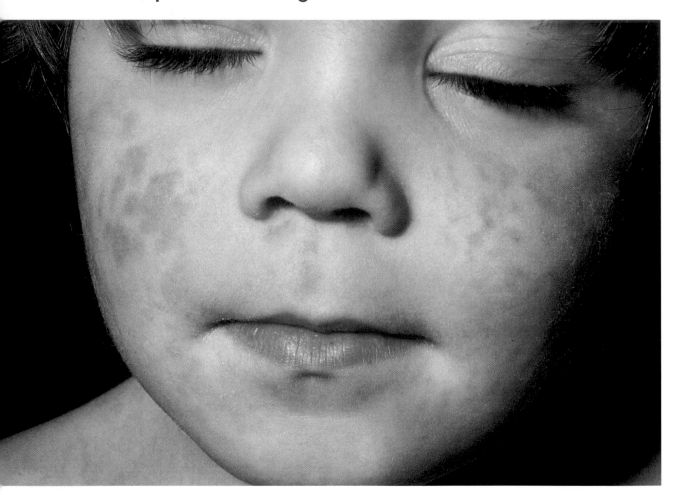

The rash may spread to your chest, stomach, arms, back, and legs. After you get the rash, you will start to feel better. You will not be **infectious** anymore.

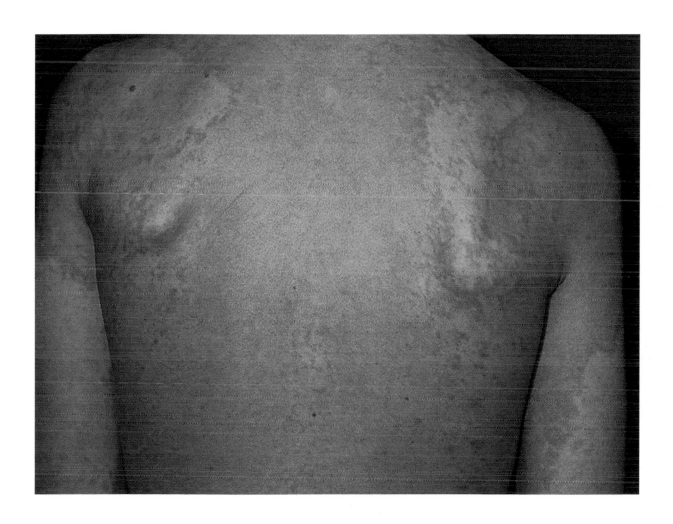

The Rash Clears Up

The **rash** lasts from one to three weeks. As the rash clears up and gets better, it looks like this. Sometimes the rash will come back before it goes away for good.

Playing outside on a warm day can make the rash come back. This is normal. It does not mean you are getting sick again.

How Fifth Disease Is Spread

Fifth disease is **infectious** only before the **rash** breaks out. It spreads when someone sneezes or coughs. Sneezing and coughing send the **virus** into the air.

You can catch fifth disease if you breathe in the virus from the air. You can also catch it if you share a cup or water bottle with a person who has fifth disease.

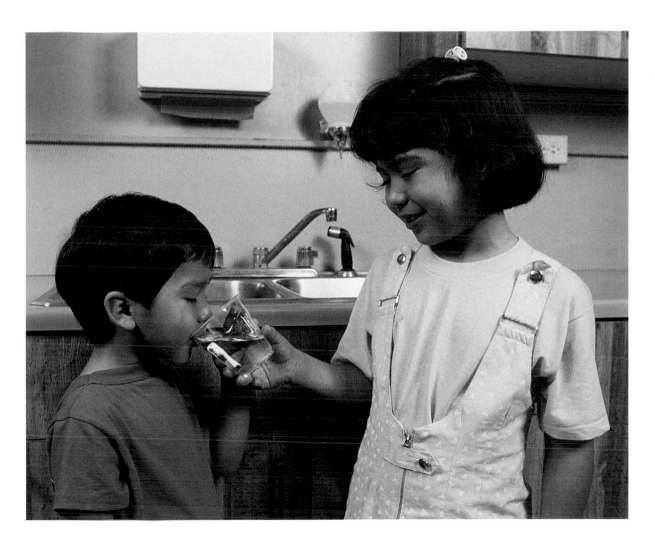

Who Gets Fifth Disease?

Anyone can get fifth disease. But most people who get fifth disease are between the ages of three and fifteen.

You can catch fifth disease any time of the year. But most people get fifth disease from late winter to early spring.

Treatment

For most people, fifth disease is not serious. If you feel tired or have a **fever,** resting at home is a good idea. Once the fifth disease **rash** breaks out, you will feel better.

The rash may itch and you might want to scratch it. An adult can give you a cream, or **ointment,** to help stop the itching.

When it's More Serious

Fifth disease is serious for people who have a sickness called **sickle cell disease.** The blood of people who have this sickness is not as healthy as other people's. Some of their red **blood cells** do not have the correct shape.

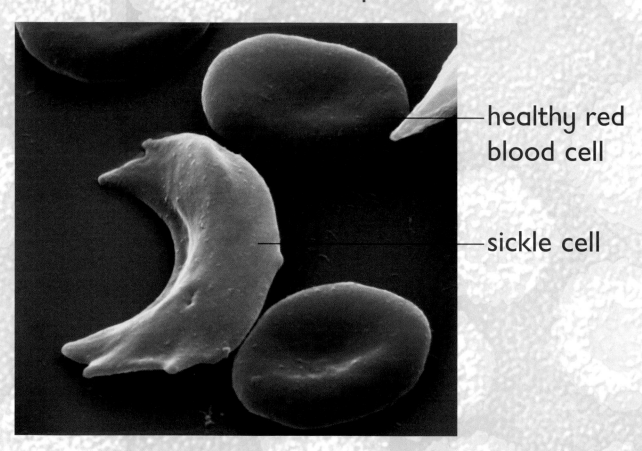

healthy red blood cell

sickle cell

Fifth disease keeps the body from making new red blood cells. If this happens to a person with sickle cell disease, they will get sick and weak. Then they will need to see a doctor.

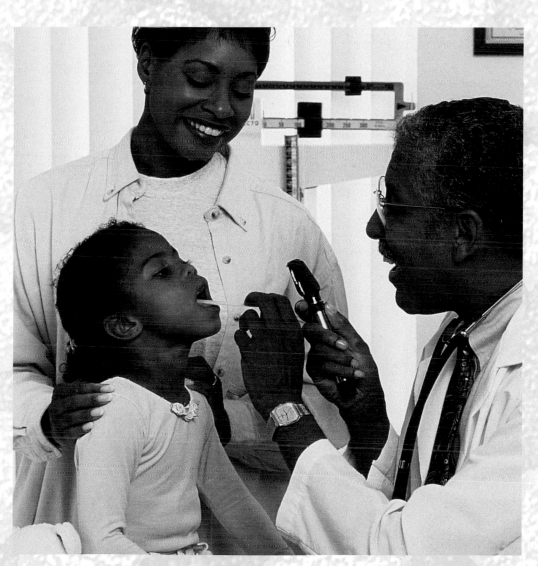

Avoiding Fifth Disease

There is no medicine that will keep you from getting fifth disease. But there are some things you can do to help keep from getting sick. You should wash your hands with soap often.

Do not share cups, knives, spoons, or forks. Try to keep your hands away from your nose and mouth. All of these things will help keep the fifth disease **virus** from getting into your body.

Staying Healthy

Once you have had fifth disease, you will have **immunity** to it. This means you cannot get it again. Your body will have made special **blood cells** like this one. These cells attack fifth disease **viruses** to keep them from making you sick.

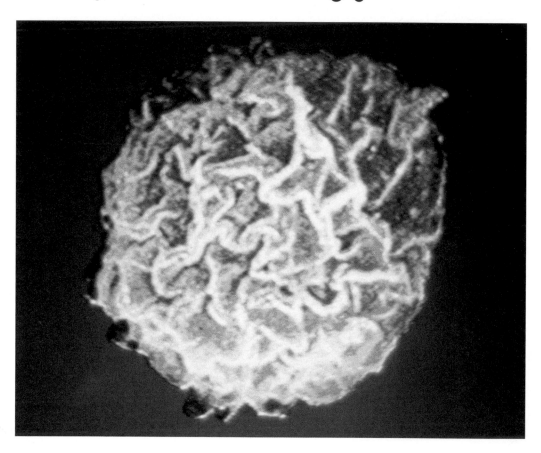

You can do your part to stay healthy.
Getting enough sleep and drinking lots
of water will help keep your body strong.
Eating healthy food is important, too.

Think about It!

Sam feels tired and has a fever and a runny nose. When will he know if he has fifth disease?*

Jay has the fifth disease **rash.** If he goes to school, will he spread fifth disease to other students in his class?*

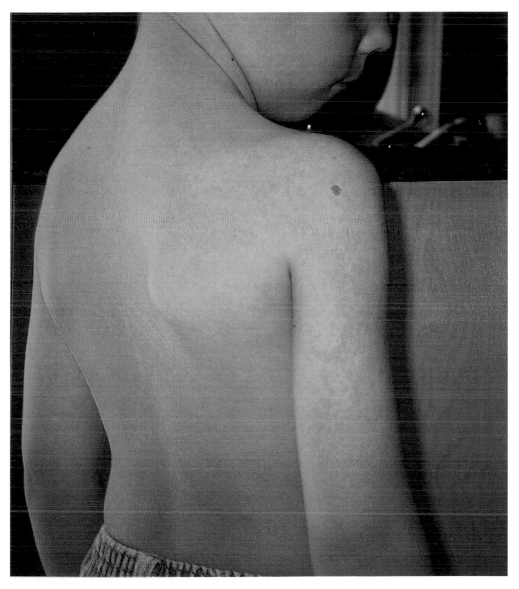

*Read page 30 to find out.

Answers

Page 28

Sam will know he has fifth disease if he gets bright red patches on his cheeks in about a week. This is the fifth disease **rash.**

Page 29

No, Jay will not spread fifth disease to his classmates. After the rash breaks out, fifth disease is no longer **infectious.**

Stay Healthy and Safe!

1. Always tell an adult if you feel sick or think there is something wrong with you.

2. Never take any medicine or use any **ointment** unless it is given to you by an adult you trust.

3. Remember, the best way to stay healthy and safe is to eat good food, drink lots of water, keep clean, exercise, and get lots of sleep.

Glossary

blood cell   very tiny part of your blood

fever   when the temperature of your body becomes hotter than normal

germ   tiny thing that can make you sick if it gets in your body

immunity   protection from getting an illness or disease

infection   illness caused by germs that can spread from one person to another

infectious   can be passed from one person to another and can make you sick

microscope   machine that makes very small things look big enough to see

ointment   cream that has medicine in it and is rubbed onto the skin

rash   red patch on the skin that often itches or is sore

sickle cell disease   illness in which some of the red blood cells, which are normally round, are shaped like the letter C

temperature   measure of how hot or cold something is

virus   tiny germ that can make you sick if it gets inside your body

Index

More Books to Read

Hundley, David H. *Viruses*. Vero Beach, Fla.: Rourke Press, 1998.

Rowan, Kate. *I Know How We Fight Germs*. Cambridge, Mass.:
    Candlewick Press, 1999.

Royston, Angela. *Clean and Healthy*. Chicago: Heinemann Library, 1999.